CEDAR HILL PUBLICATIONS

JIMMY SANTIAGO BACA

SET THIS BOOK ON FIRE!

Copyright 1999 by Jimmy Santiago Baca

First Edition

99 00 4 3 2 1

ISBN 1-891812-23-8

Several of the poems in this book have appeared in or are
scheduled for Cedar Hill Review and RATTLE Magazine.
The author wishes to thank the editors of those publications.

Publication of this book is made possible by Cedar Hill
Publications, a privately funded, self-supporting publisher
of fine poetry and a variety of other literary works. Cedar Hill
Publications is a non-subsidized, not-for-profit publishing house
which neither receives nor accepts grants of any kind.

Cover Art: Joseph "Cisk" Alvarado

Distribution: Endeavor Books, (888) 324-9303 - Toll Free
Book Manufacture: McNaughton & Gunn, (800) 677-2665

Cedar Hill Publications
3722 Hwy. 8 West
Mena, Arkansas 71953

Dedicated to

GABRIEL and ANTONIO

EDITOR'S NOTE

This book is the first installment in a trilogy of new poetry titles from Jimmy Santiago Baca. *SET THIS BOOK ON FIRE!* will be followed in May 2000 by *HAND SIGNS: Poems of an Authentic American Language. CLOSING THE CIRCLE,* the title work of the series, will appear in October 2000. Each of these books addresses specific themes the poet has spent the past five years thinking and writing about. Mr. Baca has asked me to convey to his readers and contemporaries that the reasons for many unanswered letters and phone calls are contained within the pages of this book.

On a personal note, I would like to thank the author for the opportunity to work with one of the finest poets and human beings I have encountered. I know of no one who spends more time in service to humanity than Jimmy Santiago Baca, and the fact that I am an imprisoned editor in a state of grace at this moment should be lost on no one.

Christopher Presfield
1 September 1999

CONTENTS

Part 1

Part 2

Part 3

ADDITIONAL NOTES

SET THIS BOOK ON FIRE!

Part 1

IN '78

It was prison, rioting
for our rights, burning mattresses, pounding
steel doors an inch thick,
slate, steel-painted-industrial-gray years,
fat-jowled, gut-butting, thug guards
who waddled on stumpy legs to our isolation cells
swinging batons, spraying mace, beating us
KGB fashion.

I'VE TAKEN RISKS

starting as a kid
when I stole choir uniforms
from an Episcopalian church
so I'd have something to keep me warm that winter.
I looked like a Biblical prophet
striding in six layers of robes through dark streets.

When you turned up the ace,
you kissed the card. And when the joker scoffed at you,
you were led away by authorities.
Second chances were for punks,
two-bit, jive-timing, nickel-diming
chumps.

It was beautiful in a way,
to see us kids at seven and eight
years old
standing before purple-faced authorities
screaming at us to ask forgiveness, muttering
how irresponsible we were, how impudent and defiant.

That same night
in the dark all alone, we wept in our blankets
for someone to love, to take care of us,
but we never asked for second chances.

Jimmy Santiago Baca

I'VE SEEN TOO MANY

prison catwalks with guards
cradling rifles, monitoring me,
to trust anyone, too many
barb-wired walls
to believe what people say,
looked in too many mirrors,
at too many photos
of friends and family
who died early and violently,
to believe what you say.

Understand:
all I have to be grateful for
is my little fan in summer,
my pills on the small table
where the second TV sits
with bent rabbit ears,
my empty Coors and Bud
cardboard boxes
I carry dirty laundry in
on wash day,
that window in my room
that allows me to look
out on hard streets
and dream
for a better life.

THE LIES STARTED

because who I was
couldn't take the betrayal I'd done
to those I loved, so I created a compartment
where the liar existed, a small, dark cave where
he cannibalized his heart and soul
—kept away from others—
isolating himself in a house of lies,
going into the world only to drink and drug
and fuck, waking up in the morning remembering nothing,
no words, no behavior, wallowing
in murky, alcohol grogginess that padded the wounds,
the hurts, the numbing pain of life,
how the weight got heavier with each day, each encounter,
maybe it was rage, maybe fear, maybe the inadequacy
of being flung into the world without skills
or words to communicate my heart,
how it went on, drearily fucking, faceless, bodiless,
mindless,
caught in a sordid, dizzying reel toward oblivion
until the character I created to contain
the lies, deception, drunkenness, violence,
the obscene indulgence, started
cracking the walls that separated us, crumbling
foundations, crushing the door down
until the character's venom seeped into the person
who wanted it kept away, ugly and toxic
veins of lies trickling into my clean words,
darkening my bright eyes, paling my cheeks
until I was haunted by an evil usurpation
of my being, consumed by a gluttonous appetite

Jimmy Santiago Baca

until I was what I hated, loathing myself,
all my expression fulfilling its orders
to abandon my soul, my heart,
miring myself in lies, bathing in my own foul betrayals
of all I loved and respected,
how I became a drunk, an addict, each day and every hour
my heart festering with howls for more and more
until I lived for the drug, lived to get high,
to lose myself in the darkest abyss of addiction.
Parts of myself died, crawled away into holes,
my spiritual life burned like paper in the wind,
my compassion hardened like old crumbs
of bread, and within me
the dogs of wrath and condemnation snarling, raging
day in and day out, full of contradictions,
dying and living, free and imprisoned,
feeling and insensitive, two people,
two lives guttering away
into the sewer of addiction.

THIS DARK SIDE

has always haunted me,
fiercely adamant in its opposition
to all the good I create:
subversive and defiant.
While my spirit revels in light,
it
gorges on cesspool pleasures
leaving my spirit at times a fly
and maggot-infested carcass, dissembling
my dreamwork, disintegrating it back to sand
wind scatters, blows
back into my face
I have to lower in shame.

Imagine a ladder of light, a trellis of branches
rising out of my soul in blossoming radiance,
carving its own latticed speech in the sky
toward the sun.
Imagine
my dark side freeing the termites to gnaw
down these branches.
My soul
falls like a black oak tree cracked by an ice storm.
It stares up with a skull's nightmare grimace
of cruel suffering on its frozen face.
But hovering at dawn,
hope like a butterfly floats around it,
a powdery rainbow dust effusing the air
with pervasive peace.
And then

Jimmy Santiago Baca

the morning yawns forth like whispering lilac
on the air.
My heart untangles itself from its dreams
like wild honeysuckle grandly striding into halls of sunlight,
trickling with dew beads of grace
that sigh from my lips.
Some power moves in me,
a divine dancer elegantly celebrating its existence.

I tell you now,
the dark side arrives unannounced
with cold hands,
scoffing at my efforts to live a single day in dignity,
undermining the goodness in me,
though I'm getting better at exposing it,
standing before it like a brittle twig
smashed under its wrecking tank tread.

All that I've despised and spat at in disgust
I've become at certain moments in life,
but I continue to praise the spirit,
refuse to embrace the utter horror
of self-destructive impulses.

I draw the curtains of my life shut,
a silent stranger to myself
chewing on the maddening, shredded remnants of my heart.
Accepting it as part of me, loving it,
not afraid of feeling its pain, understanding
how I always contradict myself,
I succumb to passion,
even indifference,
roar my loss and abandonment,

bell-bellow my cathedral soul,
trust and suspect
in a constant flight between light and dark.

It never ends. This harsh beauty,
this struggle not to retreat in fear
but to celebrate what's hard earned, staying true to myself,
is what it's all about.

LET ME GIVE YOU A PORTRAIT

not as pretty as uniformed La Crosse players
on an expanse of grass
in one of those
passion-drained, Ivy League schools,
a portrait
achingly real as chipped, rotted
teeth in a hobo's mouth:
direct your eyes to the peeling
picture of Saint Nino de Atocha,
that child saint who sits on a throne
with a hat with the brim turned up,
holding a staff in his left hand,
an empty reed basket in his right,
two vases of flowers before him, smiling cherubs
above circling his sacred face.
He's the one I've put through hell,
when most of my friends left,
when my boss fired me and my landlord threw me out,
when I ran out of gas one hundred miles from El Paso
and I caught my girlfriend screwing that joker,
when all I had was an opened pack of stale crackers
and dead cockroaches in the cupboard,
a jug of cold water in the icebox
for my father and brother's hangover.
Santo Nino de Atocha was there
thumb-tacked to the wall
water-stained drab green, with a medal of Our Virgin Mother
hanging over the faded retablo from a nail, veiled in blue
with hands folded, face pleading
with God to accompany this crazy boy

roaming the night streets, stealing and fighting,
and doing so I believe because
I had a pure heart, long before prison and county jail cells,
before drugs and whiskey and guns came into my life.
The pure heart I carried in me
was like a simmering volcano mouth
where roses grew and rocks talked,
where fire was my light on the hard journey,
where the journey work was staying true
to the dreams I believed in as a kid
when I folded my hands and prayed
kneeling at my cot, believing in miracles,
that angels were swirling around my shoulders,
that my dead uncles and family were present in spirit,
that no matter where I was at,
jail or streets or some forsaken, roadside motel room,
Santo Nino de Atocha accompanied me,
held my hand, guided me away from harm,
and was the reason why
the bullet missed me,
the cops ran out of breath chasing me,
I got cigarettes in the *hole* in jail,
I didn't get hurt in a fight,
I found ten bucks on the sidewalk,
I read my first volume of poetry.

THE DAY I STOPPED

being an alien to myself was that afternoon
meeting Benny at Cuco's cafe,
a familiar restaurant with Mexican soft drinks,
laborers with hip-hung, dirt-grimed jeans
and faces beaten by sun and wind
to look like real human faces.
Ordering a Coke, sipping it at the table,
I knew it was the last time I'd booze it up, get high,
knew the world around me was caving in,
saw two men on Coors fighting, saw one get shot,
the fights on the basketball court,
my own sweetness assaulted, my new change
unable to bear the sight of my old selves.
I stopped at a corner and saw a retarded woman
and her boyfriend fighting, her weeping and trying
to slice her wrist with their apartment key,
he pacing red-faced, beside himself, not knowing
how to appease her
as she sat on the bus bench whacking at her wrist,
and later this guy on the freeway honking his horn
with no one around, laying his hand on it
blasting away out of sheer insanity,
me seeing all this, worried about bills,
about confessing to my lies, deceptions,
feeling sensitive and morally healthy as I never had
knowing the time for reckoning had come,
how I had to tell it all, cleanse myself
because in all other areas I already had
preparing for my long-awaited freedom, waiting for it,
how it clawed at me where I tried to hide,

sniffed me out hungrily, demolished barricades,
the walls I'd constructed, seeing how parallel
lives I'd lived streamed around me, seeing myself
in that retarded girl, the prisoner in the back of the cop's car,
the guy madly honking his horn—too many
hotels drunk and high, with women I didn't know,
too much violence, too many
breakdowns and too much pretended happiness,
all those endless nights sweating out toxins, my body
purging the booze and drugs, screaming
its huge sense of being violated,
all those nights lying in the dark
huddled up, waiting for the torturous racks of pain
to subside, waiting to be sober, to be clean, to be true—
sheets drenched in sweat, face drawn and haggard,
eyes weak and humbled—thinking how it happened again,
how again I've fallen, again I've been ensnared,
my soul filled with evil.
I remember the last day
when I ingested drugs, how the chilling filled
my veins, my heart with corruption, venom,
how after all the work I'd done to stay clean
I'd become a sordid clown,
how that day, that very Sunday afternoon,
could be, would be, must be
the day I stopped.

I PUT ON MY JACKET

Wrapped up, I went out in winter light
climbing in volcanic rock on the west mesa
feeling softer and meaner than I've felt in years.
Amid arid scrub-brush, and bone-
biting cold, I thought of Half-Moon Bay,
how the ocean unscrolls on shore
with indecipherable messages.

Only those hiding out
from tormentors and tyrants, those in jail,
gypsies and outlaws, could understand.
The ocean talks to me
as one prisoner taps a spoon to another
through four feet of concrete
isolation-cell wall.

I HAVE ROADS IN ME

winding within my arteries
into distant hills
of memories,
where dreams float like dandelion fibers
on bright, chill, breezy
mornings under a canopy
of cottonwood branches.

Where leaves glimmer
sunlight
roads turn.

I have roads in me
where drums pound a sacrifice
and beckon
to again believe in life's wonder,
where I learn the intense passion,
seeing the sparkling, dewdripping
leaves upon moist, pine-needled ground.

My heart restored,
I am guided
by stars
and a raging desire to live.

SUNFLOWERS

How they love the murk-suck bottom
of the mother ditch
to display their arm-spread enthusiasm
for life—wish I had that
as I jog the haggard, gravel access road
parallel to the ditch. I notice
there are none on the incline
going up,
but in the murk sog and on the embankment shoulder
they wave to me. The sight of them in the clumped ooze
and on top amid seed-hefty grass
bird-tracked and curling for want of rain
wonders me.

I think of children on the playground at recess
without rule, how each gives to the other that magic space
needed to play. And it really is they
who watch me running
trying to stay healthy,
to live
to be old
after all the drugs I've put into my body
to get blazed, blitzed, drunk—
a drug-snorting, booze-guzzling,
know-it-all defiant, gutsy street-fighter
fiending for ways not to live.
They're all here waiting as they did when I was a kid,
welcoming me back to the beginning of another day,
and it wonders me.

Seeking my renewal, I gutted drug-dealer inventories
until I was an out-of-style, department-store, floor-model
mannequin
disposed of in the landfill of dark cantinas,
recycled at the drug dealer's table,
in near escapes with cops chasing me,
trigger-cocked thugs I hustled,
flipping vehicles on the roadside
passing red lights at rush hour.

Still, I'm here
in the playground of wild sunflowers
panting hard to outrun the butterfly that just passed me—
and if these are the crossroads where the living meet the dead,
I've arrived
to mourn my past, rejoice in the present,
hope for a better future,
with heaven and hell in each foot I put down
to move me on
toward the center of myself.

Jimmy Santiago Baca

COMMITMENT

A county jail guard knocked out a tooth
smacking me across the face with his club once.
I took that tooth and sharpened it on my cell floor
to an arrowhead I tied to my toothbrush with floss
to stab him with it. I never did,
but with the same commitment, I once took my brogan
and a cot-leg of angle iron
hammering it against the bars to escape, which I did.
Hammering that metal leg for months,
I finally cut that bar they said was impossible
to cut through
with a boot and cot-leg.
It's a lesson that if I can do that,
when it comes to the business of living,
I can do anything.

Part 2

IN '88

I married Beatrice,
who bore two angelic children
with hearts glistening like gold
beneath a clear, snow-melt, mountain stream.
We grew together on Black Mesa
encircled in a pool of magic light,
rippling rings of Saturn light effusing our happiness,
her laughter wild as a foal testing its legs
galloping through high alfalfa, scattering
yellow and blue blossoms in its wake,
her presence in the house
a warm refuge.

SUNDAY PRAYER

O Great Creator, I thank You
for watching over my children
and their mother, for keeping their beauty safe
and for guiding them through
all life's perilous journeys.

Give my children strength
to improve on
who they've worked so hard to be.
Gabriel's just stepping out in the world,
twelve years old and leaping high
to catch stars; clip them to his heels
like spurs as he rides his Cannondale.
Antonio seems like he's willing
to grind his feet in earth
to make his passage honorable.
I thank you for them both,
their winged spirits gentle and compassionate.

Dear Lord, keep me straight
on my path, don't let me veer.
Love me, bless me as You have,
let no harm come to my house.
Let this day be a good one,
prime the deep roots of my being
allowing them to bellow out into blossoms.
Give me the willingness to live decently,
to be a man whose acts match his words,
to think before I act, to love before I hate,
to see before my eyes are closed.

THE REASON I WAKE THIS MORNING

is because those people who've lived
through tragedies and loneliness and anxiety
found in their shattered-pottery hearts
fragments that fit perfectly
into the puzzle of night stars,
into the joyous cry
of a child at dawn
dashing out on the playground,
into the hands of men like me
who rise and dress and walk
out the door, culling from winter light
residues of summer
to dream a bit more
of the growing season.

CELEBRATE

Five hundred and five years
tortillas slapping between mamas' hands,
farmers irrigating red and green chili, squash, and corn rows,
forming halves into wholes, braiding
two roots into one thriving, ever-deepening, mother-root
bridge between black and white,
blood rainbowing
opposite shores,
connecting south to north, east to west.

Five hundred and five years
of prayers mumbled from lips,
hands clasping other hands to endure,
keeping the line intact,
unbroken hope, rosaried faith,
from Incas, Moctezuma, Cortez, Villa y Chavez,
to the anonymous men sitting on park benches
meditating on the dawn,
to women climbing cathedral steps to attend Mass,
to whimpering, wakening infants
suckling at their mothers' breasts.

Five hundred and five years
and still they remain
all beating with strong hearts,
strong
hearts celebrating the magic songs,
acts of courage that leap from them
and integrity
that shines from them.

Jimmy Santiago Baca

IN THE FOOTHILLS

of the Sangre de Cristo Mountains,
the land undulates into mound swellings and unfolding flatness
the moon seems to nest in,
settling
into scrub-brush, parched-arroyo runoffs
where as a child I believed
if we hurried we'd catch the moon,
touch the moon—it was just over the next hill:
> *Another hill, Mama! Hurry, Papa!*
> *We can still catch it!*

In the chase, my being emerged renewed,
a prairie hatchling,
to later stretch its wings and struggle free
birthing into innumerable multitudes of men,
nest within nest,
abandoning one to make another,
migrating toward seasons of laughter,
caresses, anger, troubles, joy,
and friendship.

GRANDMA

And when they come, as they have,
I seek strength in your humble memory.
As contrary and farfetched as my metaphors
and images may seem,
to a woman
in the hot, dry prairie,
when you walked, I knew
somewhere in the world a great pianist was playing
to your steps.

O dear sweet ancient woman
who never uttered a word of complaint on her behalf,
when you looked at beans, corn squash,
a simple glass of water,
your gaze held a melody of a hundred choirs
singing in harmony,
all in unison
thanking the Great Creator
for our many blessings.

I remember a woman who was
sometimes mean and cross with me,
who chased and shooed me from the house on wash day,
who made me scrub my face with freezing cold water.
Your faults were cliff-edge fingerholds
for anyone brave enough to climb to the summit
where sights could be seen only angels were given.
I climbed there many times,
and as many you called me your angel.

Jimmy Santiago Baca

Today, when I'm besieged by enemies,
when the easy way out haunts me,
when I'd prefer to sit in a cantina and drink with friends,
when doing drugs to forget the pain of living,
when I struggle to live with dignity,
when I promise to try harder,
when all my vows of conviction turn syrupy,
when the blood drains from my lips,
I kiss your face again in memory
and tell you to watch me, just watch.

I will not surrender
to the worst part of myself, Grandma.
I will be a man you can be proud of,
one who has learned well from you.
And when they come, as they do,
I'll wade out into the fields,
parting weeds, ignoring briars,
flying all these flags, hollering:
>   *Your weapons mean nothing to me,*
>   *I have Grandma in my heart!*

AT LORI'S HOUSE IN WISCONSIN

We peer into the foliage
weaving the north side of the wall,
pushing aside the tapestry of vines and tendril braidings
to view inside the robin's nest for an egg
concealed from sight.
>   *I've seen her,*
>   *but she hasn't been back in awhile,* Lori says.

The mantle of mutinous leaves and stems
is a reflection of the blazing passion of spring.
I want to keep my heart that way,
recalling a wistful sentiment
of past innocence.

So many changes happen when we fall in love.
Our days are filled with passions, supplicating our lover
for more love, more,
and as years pass the vine leaves
of our well-gardened soul chill
like beggars' rusty-edged cups
rattling against deserted-street curbs.

I toss crumbs to sparrows beneath the apple tree,
thinking of
the great concrete and iron baseball stadium in Wisconsin,
how Lori and her family took Gabe and me
to see the Brewers play,
a magical evening
of uniform composition,
from the white-chalked lines, to umpires, to players' uniforms,

---

Jimmy Santiago Baca

to the broad vista of infield and outfield clipped grass
beautiful as a bride and groom before the preacher taking vows,
the scoreboard, cheers and moans of the crowd,
hotdog hawkers and beer caterers,
me imagining
Little League kids whacking that ball,
skittering around bases—
game days
that'll never be forgotten,
just as acrobatic marvels on the monkey bars and swingsets
or that first time upturned in a canoe at the lake,
fun times
that transcend all our adult worries and broken pledges,
experiences that tune our souls
to a poetry humming, hound-howling our lives
at the moon;
how our lives fill the empty nest of each day,
brim it with mottled-egg dreams of our naive childhood
that ripen our lips like long-ago first kisses,
reddening as the years gray and wither,
and aged twigs begin to fall from the nest.

IT'S AN EASY MORNING

In the overcast sky, in those clouds
that hang over the Sandia Mountains,
a sax blows notes like raindrippings
from pine needles, darkening boulders
reminiscent of medieval churches
with worn tapestries, shimmering blue
glass altar objects, feathery
designs in the altar stonework,
making me think of loves I've lost,
loves who committed suicide—
in solemn procession through my memories
cloaked parishioners under hypnosis
carrying broken hearts to outside grottos
where the Virgin Mary smiles
out on field birds
and livestock sluggishly wakening at dawn.
I praise short lives, and believe
their souls blend into the gray
Rio Grande river, coursing between broad,
hefty cottonwoods that crowd the banks,
emptying into the ocean
where I hear them whisper
when I walk the beach,
what my expectations are,
asking if I've changed,
do I believe in God,
ebbs and tides of their voices
irreplaceably etched in my bones,
exhorting me to write
as real as the sand my feet print.

Jimmy Santiago Baca

SOMETIMES I LONG FOR MADNESS

The mystery that would spiral
my soul into a seashell
some seafaring explorer
would blow in his coming,
his arrival, his company,
his joy, his discovery.

I carry myself out in winter light
hoping music of any kind finds me,
leads me into its song,
just a note scored on paper
some child somewhere
in some faraway country
cries out at sunrise.

I MOVE THROUGH

the day in a fog, realizing
unless my fingers touch something
I'm lost. Unless I pick up a scent of coffee
or my eye catches the honeysuckle tendril blossom
swaying softly by the outside gate, my life
rattles hollow and haltingly.
I'm used to
passionate engagement, not this boredom.
Even my dog has slowed; how he used to
wander, thrashing out fowl from fields,
barking robustly, blue flames spiraling
from his ears and short tail:
he's a bird dog in a rabbit world,
and his age is starting to show in his lazy,
closing eyelids, in the way he muses
whether he should rise when I come out
with his food. Could it be this suburb we live in?
We both count the days when we can move again
by the river, well up in the mountains,
away from all this order and structure,
to piss freely in the yard, to lay back on rocks
and stare at the stars, caressing stones
as if they were a lover's hair.

Jimmy Santiago Baca

I AM UNEASY

this morning,
my heart a radar disc assaulted by strange
blips and beeps from quiet suburban streets
and cleansed, law-abiding citizens.
Even their dogs are shampooed and combed,
which I don't criticize
since mine are grungy, mean-eyed, bore-tempered,
claw-tusked mongrels
who don't give a shit at midnight: barking curs.
I suppose like me they feel ill at ease
with this altar-boy life.

One of the many defects I have
is I chew my fingernails, chewed to the cuticles,
snubbed-and-clipped, blunt buns
I nibble and yank at
unable to resist the morsel of torn flesh
or sharp fragment of fingernail,
spitting a piece out of the window,
tapping the steering wheel with bloody fingers
as I drive into the crazy city
acting like a trained, bill-paying citizen
when I'm really a bandit wanting to blow up
the Gas, Electric, and Telephone Company buildings.

THE FIRST HARD COLD RAIN

came battering
over the west mesa dunes and black volcanic rocks,
west from Gallup clattering the decrepit
shag-steer corrals. The sound of
bailing wire whipping windows
in the suburbs woke me,
and I want to thank the Lord for this
miserable morning, beautiful
in its dark raging, staining
mock-adobe, stucco-suburban two-stories
where lights in windows flick on
and responsible parents rise
to breakfast and work.

I've been anything but responsible,
neglecting laws, cursing authority,
jeering meatless, ham-bone statesmen,
spewing my gangland rhetoric
cloaked in a smile
for cookie-jar enticements
and dinner bells ringing beans,
chili, and tortillas, but that's not what makes
this morning so miserable.
You see, after the smoking,
teenaged, snub-nosed days cool,
and I find myself
comfortable in my destruction
and shortfall of accomplished goals,

the serpentine, blue-scaled rain snaps

Jimmy Santiago Baca

the screen door and pops chimney tin,
shimmering streets I look out on through my window
in t-shirt and underwear. Memories
of old friends sharing Tokay wine
in Texas barns on alfalfa bales
come back to me, or traveling
in that beat-up car
when sunrise over Big Bend cliffs
made me believe in miracles
big as Texas. Realize:
I don't need to be what you expected I should be,
nor apologize for my cat-burglarizing days
or my raccoon-pilfering-dog-food-
from-the-bowl-on-the-porch ways. Realize:

on dark, rainy mornings like this, men like me
are nothing more than birds in a fruit tree
they tried to chase away.
But we got to bite the ripest fruit first,
spoiled the farmer's weekend at the grower's market
when he had to explain to customers about them damn birds
that got his fruit, trying everything to keep us away
from gorging on life. We
who refused to be caged canaries
didn't mind getting our feathers wet
just to feel what it might be like
to fly into the storm.

Storm-ravaged, that's the image I was looking for
when I said goodbye to my son this morning
as he was leaving for school,
my youngest still asleep in bed, when I made space
for my children to start their journey.

I don't mind this miserable, cold rain
so beautiful in its discomfort,
its sweet ravage familiar to me
from those steel-toed, heel-rocking,
bloody-knuckle years when I rode
at night through the Sandia Mountains
whurrumphing my Harley, gattling-gunned back,
throttling for a taste of real life,
to fly like a bird. Call it art,
antisocial. I call it love.

Part 3

IN '98

How all the beauty
ended up out
on the garden trellis
like an unused fishing net,
my dreams rusting, red tricycles
in backyard weeds,
dry-docked old boats on bricks,
stray dogs chasing cars
that keep getting hit.

GHOST READING IN SACRAMENTO

For days I feel a ghost
trailing me, memories aching and joyous,
from kitchen to basketball courts
to walking paths to driving around town,
a presence hovers about me
like the incipient, tight-furled rosebud
on the verge of breaking free, and I realize
miracles come in colors, soft bruises—
the mean scowl of a drunk
in a corner booth in a bar,
the elation a kid feels freed
of morning chores, leaping and running
out to the playground. I feel startled,
surrounded by memories,
like one of those sailors who finally comes ashore
to kneel before a humble altar, surrendering to feelings
that the world is too large for him to see it all, a man
whose heart once radiated stamina, strength, and firmness
yet now like a sail is folded to the mast:
from Charlie whirling in old songs
mimicking oldies but goodies
to Gilbert's miner's grubbing for gold
in his coal-shaft past
to your solitary dance
in a room filled with dreams
to David's hunting through jungles of cells
tracking a cure for AIDS
to that guy in Sacramento
who made us all realize something more beyond ourselves,
who drew our thinking out of our eyes

Jimmy Santiago Baca

in tears, his voice a sudden catching,
kindling and flame,
reminding us of our own flickering journey.

THE TRUTH BE KNOWN

I quit writing to study cooking,
to learn how to make a delicious tortilla,
to devote my time to creating magnificent gardens,
fragrant, enchanting patios for friends
designed with the moon and stars in mind.

Down at the San Jose Community Center,
I shoulder a satchel brimming with poems
I've composed to teach kids how to read and write.
I buy them pizza and soda,
to make writing a pleasurable experience,
associate it with food, friendship, and laughter.

The next morning I wander store aisles,
reading book spines, searching for poetry
to give to adults pursuing their GEDs,
but the poetry either lionizes the poet
as a savior of Mexicans
crossing the border
or makes the images so exotic
it compares the ordinary fork and spoon
with dormant volcanoes,
losing my attention in the process.

We need a shoe to be a shoe,
for the poet to describe the foot
inside, the miles walked, the weariness
that seeps into toes, heel, and calf,
the tired dreams those feet lug every day.

Jimmy Santiago Baca

I return to my abandoned cabin,
become a wild man
dancing Irish jigs to nature,
babbling nonsensical Yeats rhymes to myself.

POETS CAN STILL HAVE A GOOD HEART

and have a past riddled with violence,
a strong heart and have known addiction,
a good heart and have known drunks and thieves.
Do this: stand
before a group of Uppidees,
admit you know someone with AIDS,
someone in prison,
someone homeless,
someone with mental illness,
someone handicapped.
It means
while most turn away their hearts
you face life, use the sweet impulse of pulsing blood
to live your life,
not to live a lie.

I'm in the garden this morning
pleased the roses are so bountiful,
awed by the lilac's treasure of fragrance,
honeysuckle vines flourishing,
climbing over each other up the wall
toward sunrays, shivering with hungry freedom
for the open-road radiance.
I don't remember my dreams this morning
but keep a journal next to my bed in case I do.
Its empty pages welcome images, voices
sifted and tunneled through my waiting pen.
I intend
to compose poems
of friends who died in recent years.

I keep talking to them, hearing them in my head,
admirable acquaintances I wish to honor,
ones who stood, who labored against oppression
with heels dug in dirt against retreat:
voices, brilliant comets
subverting the dark.

IT MAKES SENSE TO ME NOW

That evening
I drove down from San Francisco to Los Angeles
and dropped in to visit Luis,
who told me:
      It's your turn to carry the torch.

Years later
the significance of those words
flared like a stick-match in the dark
the day Paz gave me a painting
of Nahuatl Dancers
tethered by the ankles, who fly
around the pole.
The lead Dancer, El Maestro, stands on top:
he's back from visiting the sun,
bearing a message for us on earth.

At dawn
I make my way downstairs
to make coffee, nodding
my respects to El Maestro:
bunches of flowers on his hat,
yellow/red/green/blue headband tassels
ribbon out in wind.
He beats a small drum and blows his flute,
a single eagle flaps by clouds behind him
as he balances on the pole;
the reddening, orange-gold sky ablaze
with light.
I wonder what his message is

and how it pertains to me.

Now
I drive twice a week to San Jose barrio
volunteering to teach reading and writing,
and I remember

one evening
I asked the children and parents to write a letter poem
describing their journey to America:
risking lives, homes burned, fleeing death squads
after husbands and brothers were murdered,
the women raped. I'll never forget

when
this little girl, too shy to read aloud
her praise and love for her mother,
had me sit on the floor next to her
as she stood on a makeshift stage
in a bookstore. When she uttered that first word
a glint of light sparked across her brown eyes
into the world, as if it were golden
speech without sound. I sat amazed
at the light in her eyes, igniting a memory in me—

when
I too recited my first poem. The intensity and radiance of
a child reaffirmed my original reason for writing,
one I'd forgotten along the way.

Suddenly
I knew, keeping the light intact,
not teaching writing, not to mold or direct,

just to keep it burning, blowing on the embers
so hope doesn't go out,
that was the message El Maestro was bringing me
from the sun.

I WISH MY LIFE

fit the day's needs
as coal in winter or ice in summer. You never know
when you're signing for your happiness
you're not signing your execution papers.
More incredible's
how folks use faith in God
to ignore the starving, to be
indifferent to the homeless, assume
God will punish those who locked the boxcar
suffocating those Mexicans locked inside
like the human beings who rot in prison.

I'm called spic, wetback, illegal alien
because there is a god.
And if I get paid what I've earned, deserve for honest labor,
another law is drafted to keep me a slave
while preferential treatment and advantage are given
to the rich calling the shots.

I don't mean to be insolent, to sound pontifical,
but I know
nonsense
when I hear it.
Instance:
at UNIversities
where professors are more Uppidee
than a stretch of snowy Kansas field,
rarely do they trust Chicanos or Indios to teach,
only those with rug-burned knees.
Instance:

Governor of Arizona, found GUILTY of a slew of felonies,
airs his grief before a press conference, quoting
from the Bible
how prophets are often considered lepers in their own town.
Now come on, I'm thinking,
this is getting too strange.

Were I to speak out
on the absurdities,
like Jordan making more in five-second sound bites
for NIKE
than thousands of rank-and-file workers in a year,
I'd be glared down, accused of race baiting,
diagnosed a danger to myself, committed
to the unspoken
BLACK LIST.

I've heard gibberish
from friends living in gorgeous coastal homes,
driving deluxe Beamers,
the bark and arf-arf of their buried-bone bits of beliefs:
>   *You're a danger to yourself.*
>   *Ask the Holy Spirit to heal you.*
>   *God is free, independent of all nations,*
>   *not funded by the state, not subject to king.*
But when I ask them for donations to buy books
for disadvantaged children, they reply:
>   *I give my gift basket at Christmas*
>   *through the church.*
I guess there's room for all kinds in this life.

THE JOURNEY HAS ALWAYS BEEN

what we didn't do or did, how far we've come
to a place
where dream fragments smolder:
hot pebbles cooling after a summer rain.

It happens I am a singer of the heart
and took my songs to the gutter to sing them to drunks,
recite them to addicts,
whisper them to thieves and madmen,
outstretch them like my hands
clasping prisoners' hands
through cell bars.

You see, it's these people who understand the poem's magic,
who are not invited into society,
whose opinions we denigrate as useless,
but each unlike Uppidees fight hard for their existence,
battle against armed keepers to speak, stand, and breathe.

They've known the blessing light of the poem
on their trampled hearts,
the poem's respite in a merciless society,
its sensory indulgence in their own severe deprivations,
its love and respect
away from the mockery, ridicule, and shame
that accusers heap on them.

The poem's words
scrub away the rust on their hearts
drawing out the burnished luster of their dreams,

---

and radiates a certain light from their bones.
As they roam the murky alleys,
it transforms their suffering into songs of celebration,
strengthening their convictions
to stay when ordered out.

Commanded to sit, they stand.
Asked to speak, they withdraw into silence.
They are, in other words,
true to the poem,
loyal to the heart,
merging the two.

MY DOG BARKS

Come close, listen: at the door a professor from Flagstaff asks
can I participate in a conference on prison writing.
I decline. Conferences are squeamish about truth.
If your words don't fit their theories,
if you claim that convicts are people,
that writing goes deep in the soul, to memories,
to flesh and blood, that writing has more to do
with cruel guards and torture chambers, isolation cells
and chained beatings, they become squeamish.

I know a man
in Patterson, New Jersey; the guy
wasn't allowed to write a letter
to his wife after she had their child,
so he hid himself away and wrote
a poem in blood.

I visited the house where Thoreau lived once,
where he wrote of the oppressed and murdered in prison,
how they're imprisoned because they're poor,
how they have human rights. He wrote
about humanity, not just about writing
as with those whose work seems detached
from their own hearts, not like the conference types
who believe there is no way to help
the imprisoned, that it's best to keep them in
while having workshops on prison writing.

I talk back, think individually;
this is strictly a conference on writing

---

in prison, and if you had writers who'd been cons
it would make the conference a success.
But you don't want to hear what they're going through,
you prefer to translate their suffering into MFA papers,
to turn their deaths into metaphors,
to make their real cries and real terror a tone in the text
that people outside can philosophize about;
it's only about writing, not what would free these men
from their tormentors. Besides, if they weren't in prison
you wouldn't be able to have a conference, would you?

Come close, listen: I decline the offer
to pander to suspicions,
decline not to discuss what drives the writing,
what the writing really means,
what it means to be a writer in prison in the first place,
not some yahooing convict with a book
whose fame is built on kissing ass.
And while I'm at it, I decline your myth of censorship,
where every bookstore in the city prints
handouts about some fool in Podunk or New York
burning a book: that's not censorship, that's bullshit!

The writing conference definition of censorship
will hail the work of some gawkish clown
who's never been behind bars—portray him as a victim.
Or take that girl born into uppercrust, tsst-tsst
murmurings. After doing a book on the border,
right away she's a heroine of the underclass,
jailed entirely for symbolic purposes.
O how they offer their wrists to the cop!

Come close, listen: the real definition of censorship

is when they keep you locked in the *hole*
for ninety days without light or exercise
so you have to compose your poems in your head
and remember them. The real definition
of a prison writing program
is when a prisoner has to write
a poem in blood.

ANOTHER POET I'VE KNOWN

This woman I honor, respect, am blessed to have as friend,
who picked me up at O'Hare Airport in Chicago,
who'd been through everything
unimaginable, enduring it,
growing like a blueberry tree, more leafy
grace in her gestures, her rotund
laughter, heady
with mysterious gaiety in her eyes.
Raped once by four policemen,
her man murdered by the FBI,
she retreated
into deep, green mountains with her daughter
to retrieve
that crystalline innocence
of the dewdrop in her tears,
to douse the flames of her agony.

Yes, I've known a woman
who took me from Chicago to Milwaukee, who I thanked
for picking me up,
who drove three hours late at night, renting a new truck
because her car was too old and might break down,
who worked ten times harder than any tenured professor
while getting paid half her worth, half
what her male counterparts made.
I remember her at the table
with students of every race, color,
seeing how they respected her, how she lavished
attention on them.
Not one award,

no plaque of distinction, not one NEA
grant adorning her walls, a commoner
of the sort who make the real world habitable.

Her spirit splendor mists my loneliness,
the kind of luminosity I see hovering
at the river's banks, burning away at sunrise
disclosing landscaped fields, bright streams, mountains.
She was that for me, this poet living
in her small apartment with her doves, parakeets, and plants,
Christmas lights nailed above the kitchen doorway,
rising early to make tortillas for students, guests,
creating cards to send to friends
splendid and elaborate as Diego Rivera, collages
sprouting in her hands like seeds
in soil moist as farmers' field rows.
Blessed I am
to have known this woman, blessed
I am to be her friend, this angel
who said of her life:
          It's a Chicago thing.

Frida Kahlo's brow, her eyes,
lush hair, sensual hips and breasts.
Paintings hang in every room,
stations of the cross she recorded
on her journey
from hell to the mountain peak,
cherished faces of the people she loved
in the center of her bleeding heart.
I'm awed by her healing, like magic
that deep, raucous laughter bordering each day,
her life a pine forest

abundant with eagles, fragile creeks,
a solace to weary travelers like me.

Just a woman,
mother, painter, and teacher,
another poet I've known.

WITH PAZ BY THE FIRE LAST NIGHT

We talk about the warrior's journey
when suddenly he looks up, and says:
           It's the rage I have trouble with.
I wake and have my coffee, write,
go to the mesas to walk in canyons.

I admire the layered clouds, winter light in sage,
find a campsite littered with shotgun-shell casings,
plastic bottles and canisters riddled with buckshot
an outlaw hangout for gun lovers.
I cut and floor the pedal
bouncing out on the dirt road
and see a couple walking their dog,
realizing how life keeps reminding me
I'm doing what I should be.

A phone call from a woman needing help,
a reading by an ex-con who memorized my *Crying Poem,*
a small speech I gave for the New York premiere of
a new documentary on adult literacy,
a benefit for Leonard Peltier's defense fund,
a meeting with Fortune Society members
to talk about making it on the streets—
the soul is what matters, how drugs infest the soul
with diseased, cancerous muck
that must be scraped away, cleaned off with prayer,
the sheer work of living healthy.

Tutoring barrio families to read and write,
volunteering my services with joy,

---

always rushed and exhausted, I move into winter light
that invigorates my resilience
to endure the betrayals of haughty, Ivory Tower
intellectuals, academics with all that
musky ineffectualness hunkered down in booklined offices
trading the classroom in for festivals in the park.

I cry into the mike for commitment,
avoiding journalists, TV reporters, interviews or articles;
calling Guadalupe in the mountains
to deliver wood to impoverished families
whose only source of heat is fire.
At dawn I tread rocky trails
breathing in cold air, absorbed
in the phosphorescent brilliance
of dew and cold on sage stems.

The winter light remains
a written testimony on my journey
to clouds and light and shadows
always moving, rearranging, rushing
into canyon crevices.
The phone is ringing, the letters stack up,
bills need to be paid, my children attended,
a novel and various manuscripts edited.

Sensitive friends drop by with booze and drugs
to shock to life their own dead systems.
I note the signs every day
that I'm moving forth
alone into winter light,
into a place where flowers grow in snow
and tears are made in flames.

Looking back on a broken marriage
and substance abuse, I see it as a time
when locusts swarmed across my heart
eating away the nurturing marrow of green life
and leaving a wake of dust-bowl bleakness,
a shadow of a man holding his brimmed hat on his head
fiercely leaning into howling gusts,
roadless, mapless, stung and pelleted,
a shriveled, gaunt, life-starved skeleton,
each day's casket closed, submerged in oblivion.

I find myself meandering a coastline
observing the gulls ride waves gracefully,
shimmery feathers tucked into their sides;
in the distance fog wraps mountain peaks
and coves quell in peaceful slumber;
my footfalls leave deep imprints in moist sand
where I see tides sucked in and vanish.
I imagine grief goes that way,
that change comes like the ebb,
a playground teeter-totter
or windblown, child's swing at dusk.

The wind rides the swings,
lifts and drops the teeter-totter.
Amid screaming divorcees
and lung-cancer patients,
a lone gull alights on a log
left after the flood
that hurled refrigerators a mile downstream,
backfilled rooms to ceilings with mud,
juggled and tossed entire homes
to smithereens against cliff banks.

I see how fragile plants endure,
how they bulk with weighty blossoms,
and I understand the beauty of gulls
in winter light, riding cold waves,
taking no provisions for their journey,
no map or army or money,
no crude baggage from the past.

They dive into a blue, ethereal reef-world
and the sea caresses them
like a loving hand behind a dog's ear,
who shakes awake and barks to go outside
where dewy frost burns off in sunlight
that warms the bones of travelers,
who long ago lost their dreams and now have only stories
of loneliness and love, danger and courage,
to tell around the fire beneath the stars.

Jimmy Santiago Baca

SET THIS BOOK ON FIRE!

Rising
in the glow of the embers,
and even in the ashes, I want to tell you:
I've spent years
studying stark cries in the cancerous marrow
of inner-city streets. I've gone to
Uppidee districts to witness poets
who kiss their asses while adjusting grins,
luring audience approval with politically correct quips.

I want to tell you:
don't lie! If you're going to read a poem
about a kid getting his head blown off,
don't raw jaw your cotton-tipped tongue
to gain the sugary aplomb and donut favor
of English Department heads, who like you
and never scavenged food from dumpsters, who like you
and never stood in welfare lines, who like you
while gleaning misery topics from *The New York Times.*

I want to tell you:
if you're going to preach what you don't follow,
testify to what you haven't lived,
hoola-hoop your way like a pride-plucked hen
doormatting your heart for moneyed admirers
whose concerned faces ooh and ahh faked empathy,
know that poetry deserves better than that
hee-hawing, educated, hillbilly-mule
whinnying for the crowd response.

I want to tell you:
while you do your sheepish, poor-me routine,
your victim-in-distress sighing,
poor people are being murdered,
prisoners are being zapped with fifty thousand volts
of electricity to make them behave.
O hollow-hearted, New-Age activist that you are,
tell us in your poetry how coolly you've risked
your life helping refugees cross the border.

I want to tell you:
what you're looking for is a new title to acclaim,
what you want is to be hailed a savior
when you spice your poetry with theatrics,
crumpling on the floor and groaning with rage.
O how the world has done you wrong!
The last thing we need is more toothless tigers
stalking thousand-dollar checks from sympathetic patrons
of first-class airlines and four-star hotels.

I want to tell you:
I'm weary of these castrated Uppidees,
poets and patrons who've hardly engaged in life.
I'm tired of the prejudice they never own,
tired of them spouting off familiar remedies
to a world of ills they've never known.
I beg you both, get out of the way,
please step aside, just a couple of steps,
it takes too much effort to go around you.

I want to tell you:
the flashpoint of paper is 451 degrees.

WHY AND WHEN AND HOW

did our lives move from the page
words composed so elegantly
boy's choirs could harmonize,
how did they scatter
like crumbs on the floor
swept up
and tossed from our lives
to decompose with the rest,
how did our pastoral
move from the canvas
to join the mob in madness
when we dreamed we heard angels
whisper once in our sleep?

ADDITIONAL WORKS

HAND SIGNS: Poems of an Authentic American Language

Book II of the CLOSING THE CIRCLE trilogy. In the tradition of Pablo Neruda, Mr. Baca combines stunning lyrical intensity with pointed commitment to America's dispossessed. Available in May 2000 from Cedar Hill.

CLOSING THE CIRCLE

Book III of the trilogy. CLOSING THE CIRCLE delves deep into the roots of Chicano culture in the American southwest, inspired by the vision of a Native American shaman. Available in October 2000 from Cedar Hill.

ABOUT THE AUTHOR

Jimmy Santiago Baca was born in Santa Fe, New Mexico in 1952. His books of poetry include IMMIGRANTS IN OUR OWN LAND, BLACK MESA POEMS, MARTIN AND OTHER MEDITATIONS ON THE SOUTH VALLEY, and THE EROTIC POEMS. As a screenwriter and film producer, his credits include BOUND BY HONOR, BLOOD IN BLOOD OUT, MEXICAN ROOTS, THE PANCHO GONZALES STORY, and EL CHAMACO. His awards include the NATIONAL ENDOWMENT FOR POETRY AWARD, VOGELSTEIN FOUNDATION AWARD, NATIONAL HISPANIC HERITAGE AWARD, BERKELEY REGENTS AWARD, PUSHCART PRIZE, SOUTHWEST BOOK AWARD, and AMERICAN BOOK AWARD. He lives with his two children in Albuquerque, New Mexico.

CEDAR HILL PUBLICATIONS
3722 Hwy. 8 West
Mena, Arkansas 71953

GUTTERSNIPE CANTICLE—Amelia Raymond
    $9.00–Poetry
    ISBN 1-891812-22-X

SUBURBAN LIGHT—William Doreski
    $10.00–Poetry
    ISBN 1-891812-16-5

THE SILK AT HER THROAT—James Doyle
    $10.00–Poetry
    ISBN 1-891812-12-4

96 SONNETS FACING CONVICTION—Leonard J. Cirino
    $10.00–Poetry
    ISBN 1-891812-20-3

PROVERBS FOR THE INITIATED—Kenn Mitchell
    $11.00–Poetry
    ISBN 1-891812-06-8

THE BOOK OF ALLEGORY—Michael McIrvin
    $10.00–Poetry
    ISBN 1-891812-03-3

AMNESIA TANGO—Alan Britt
    $10.00–Poetry
    ISBN 1-891812-14-9

7th CIRCLE—Maggie Jaffe
    $10.00–Poetry
    ISBN 1-891812-07-6

NEXT EXIT—Taylor Graham
    $10.00–Poetry
    ISBN 1-891812-13-0

PIECES OF EIGHT: A Women's Anthology of Verse
    $10.00–Poetry
    ISBN 1-891812-02-5

JAM: Cedar Hill Anthology Series
    $10.00–Poetry
    ISBN 1-891812-05-X

BODY AND SOUL—Sharon Doubiago (forthcoming - Spring 2000)
    $15.00–Poetry
    ISBN 1-891812-24-6

Available from: http://www.amazon.com/